Mother Teresa

by Candice F. Ransom
illustrations by Elaine Verstraete

Carolrhoda Books, Inc./Minneapolis

Carolrhoda Books, Inc.
A division of Lerner Publishing Group
241 First Avenue North
Minneapolis, MN 55401 U.S.A.

Website address: www.lernerbooks.com

Library of Congress Cataloging-in-Publication Data

Ransom, Candice F., 1952–
    Mother Teresa / by Candice F. Ransom; illustrations by Elaine Verstraete.
        p. cm. — (On my own biography)
    ISBN 1-57505-441-8 (lib. bdg.: alk. paper)
    1. Teresa, Mother, 1910–1997—Juvenile literature. 2. Missionaries of Charity—Biography—Juvenile literature. [1. Teresa, Mother, 1910–1997. 2. Missionaries of Charity. 3. Missionaries. 4. Nuns. 5. Nobel Prizes—Biography. 6. Women—Biography.] I. Verstraete, Elaine, ill. II. Title. III. Series.
BX4406.5.Z8 R36   2001
271'.97—dc21   00-009396

Manufactured in the United States of America
1 2 3 4 5 6 – JR – 06 05 04 03 02 01

To Jeanne, a true believer
                              —C. F. R.

For my mother
      and
For my sister
              —E. V.

Skopje, Albania

1919

When Mother Teresa was a girl,
her name was Agnes Bojaxhiu.
Agnes loved market day.
She followed her mother, Drana,
around the bazaar.

4

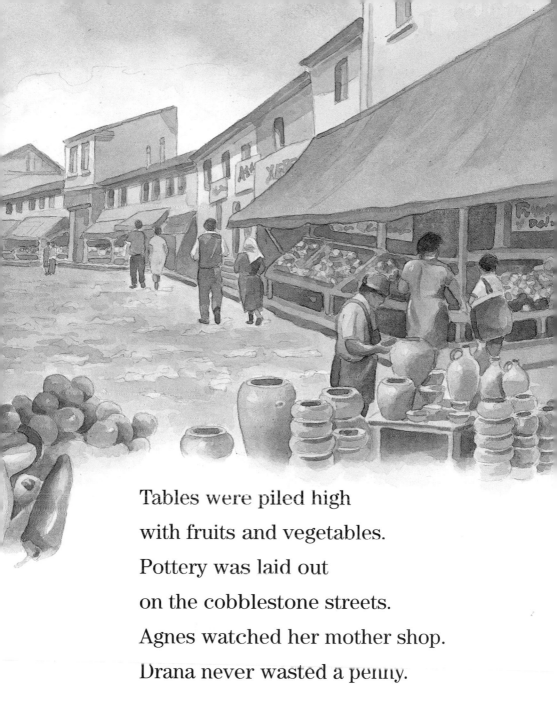

Tables were piled high
with fruits and vegetables.
Pottery was laid out
on the cobblestone streets.
Agnes watched her mother shop.
Drana never wasted a penny.

It had been a hard year.

Agnes's father had died.

Nine-year-old Agnes missed her father.

He had called her "Flower Bud."

Her sister, Age,

and brother, Lazar, missed him, too.

He had been a wealthy businessman.

Without him, the Bojaxhiu family was poor.

So Drana opened a shop.

She embroidered cloth and sold it.

She sewed wedding dresses

and costumes for festivals.

Back at home, a knock sounded at the door.

A poor woman stood there.

Drana asked the woman
to eat dinner with them.

So the woman joined Agnes, Age, Lazar,
and their mother at the table.
Agnes thought the woman was a relative.
But she was a stranger.
Drana told Agnes hungry strangers
should never be turned away.

When a neighbor got sick,
Agnes and her mother went to care
for the woman.
They washed and fed her twice a day.
They also helped a widow
who had six children.
When Drana had to work,
Agnes went by herself.
Like her mother,
Agnes believed in helping others.

Skopje, Albania

1922

Twelve-year-old Agnes lifted her voice
in joy.
She loved to sing in the church choir.
Lazar teased her.
He said she spent more time
at Sacred Heart Church than at home.

12

Agnes went to school at Sacred Heart.

Lazar and Age had gone there, too.

Agnes was a quiet student.

She liked working at the church

with her mother.

They picked flowers for festivals.

They hung banners and flags for pageants.

Agnes was happy,
but she wasn't always well.
She often caught coughs and fevers.
The damp winters were not good
for her health.
So in the summer,
her family went to the mountains.
The mountains had fresh air
and clean, tumbling streams.

In the mountains, Agnes prayed
at the statue of the Madonna of Letnice.
She and Age took long walks.
At night, they told stories
around the big fireplace.
Agnes was happiest of all on these trips.

The summer Agnes was 12,

something happened.

Agnes went to the statue.

She lit her candle and prayed.

As she prayed, she heard a voice.

The voice told her to follow God

and to serve others.

God had spoken to her!

Agnes knew what she must do with her life.

She would help the poor.

She would devote her life to the church

and become a nun.

Calcutta, India

1931

Sister Teresa stood in front
of her classroom.

Her name wasn't Agnes anymore.

For years, she had trained to be a nun.

That spring, she had taken her first vows.

She promised to give up many things.

She must live and work
inside the convent walls.
She couldn't marry or have a family.
When Agnes became a nun,
she took a new name.
She chose the name Saint Teresa of the
Little Flower.
From that day on, she was Sister Teresa.

19

Sister Teresa was happy
teaching at the Loreto Convent school.
She looked out the window
at the wide green lawns.
All was peaceful.
There was enough to eat.
But life was far from peaceful
outside Loreto's walls.

The Loreto Convent was in Calcutta,
a city called "the City of Palaces."
Calcutta was also a shocking place,
with crowded, dirty areas called slums.
Poor people lived on the streets.
Children wore rags and ate garbage.
Sister Teresa had become a nun
in a poor country.
She had followed God's calling.
But something was missing.

Six years later,

Sister Teresa took her final vows.

She promised to be poor.

She promised to obey God.

Soon after, she became the principal
at Loreto's school.

She had nearly 300 girls in her care.

When war broke out in India,
Sister Teresa was worried.

Food was scarce.

The streets rang with gunfire.

Tanks rumbled by.

Men climbed over the convent walls
to escape the riots.

Sister Teresa helped them.

Trucks usually brought food to Loreto.

But they couldn't get through the riots.

The school had no food.

For the first time in years,

Sister Teresa went outside Loreto's walls.

Everywhere she looked,

she saw people who were wounded or dead.

She saw the poor people

who lived on the streets.

Then she spotted a jeep with sacks of rice.

A soldier tried to stop her.

But Sister Teresa got her rice.

Safely back at Loreto, she couldn't forget

the sights outside the walls.

Eastern India

September 10, 1946

A month later, Sister Teresa sat on a train.

She was going to the mountains,

far from the heat and slums of Calcutta.

The fresh air would give her a rest.

The train wheels went *click-a-clack*.

Sister Teresa prayed.

Over the train wheels, she heard a voice.

God told her to leave Loreto.

He wanted her to go into the slums.

He wanted her to serve the poor.

Sister Teresa was surprised.

She hadn't thought God would speak to her again!

But she knew she needed to work directly with the poor.

This was what had been missing from her life.

Back in Calcutta, Sister Teresa prepared to leave the convent.

It was hard to say good-bye.

Sister Teresa had been at the convent for 20 years.

She loved teaching there.

But she had to answer God's call.

Sister Teresa left the safe walls of Loreto
with only a few coins.
Her nun's habit was too hot.
She bought a sari,
the dress worn by Indian women.
It was cheap white cotton
with three blue stripes.
She draped it around her
and pinned a cross on her left shoulder.
Sister Teresa needed to get
medical training.
Many people on the streets were sick.
They needed medical care.

So Sister Teresa visited nuns
who knew how to give medical care.
She learned how give first aid.
She watched operations.
She helped mothers with childbirth.
Sister Teresa told the nuns she wanted
to care for the poorest of the poor.
She would live with the poor.
She would eat what they ate—only rice.
But one nun told Sister Teresa
she must stay healthy.
She must eat well, rest, and stay clean.
Then she would have the energy
to help the poor.
Sister Teresa knew the nun was right.

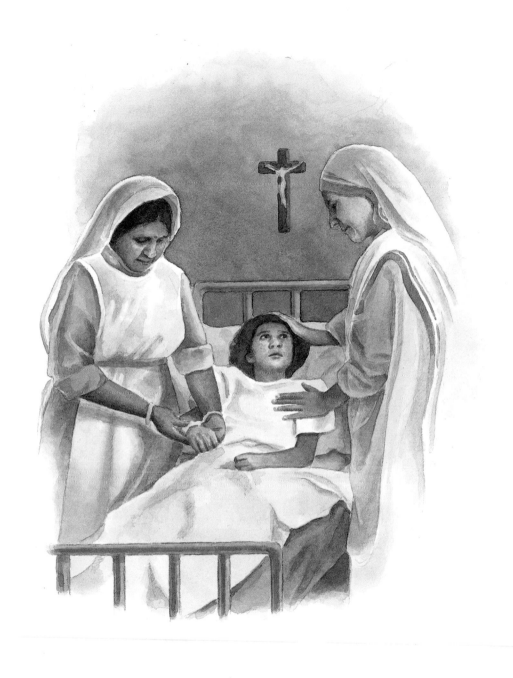

Calcutta, India

1948

Near the Loreto School was a slum

called Moti Jihl.

The name meant "Pearl Lake."

But the slum didn't look

like the beautiful name.

People lived in huts with mud floors.

They drank and bathed in a filthy pond.

The small nun in a white sari
walked into the slum.
What should she do first?

Sister Teresa was a teacher.

So she started a school.

Sister Teresa gathered children

under a locust tree.

With a stick, she wrote letters in the dirt.

The next day, someone gave her a chair.

Then came a table.

Soon many children were learning

in Sister Teresa's open-air school.

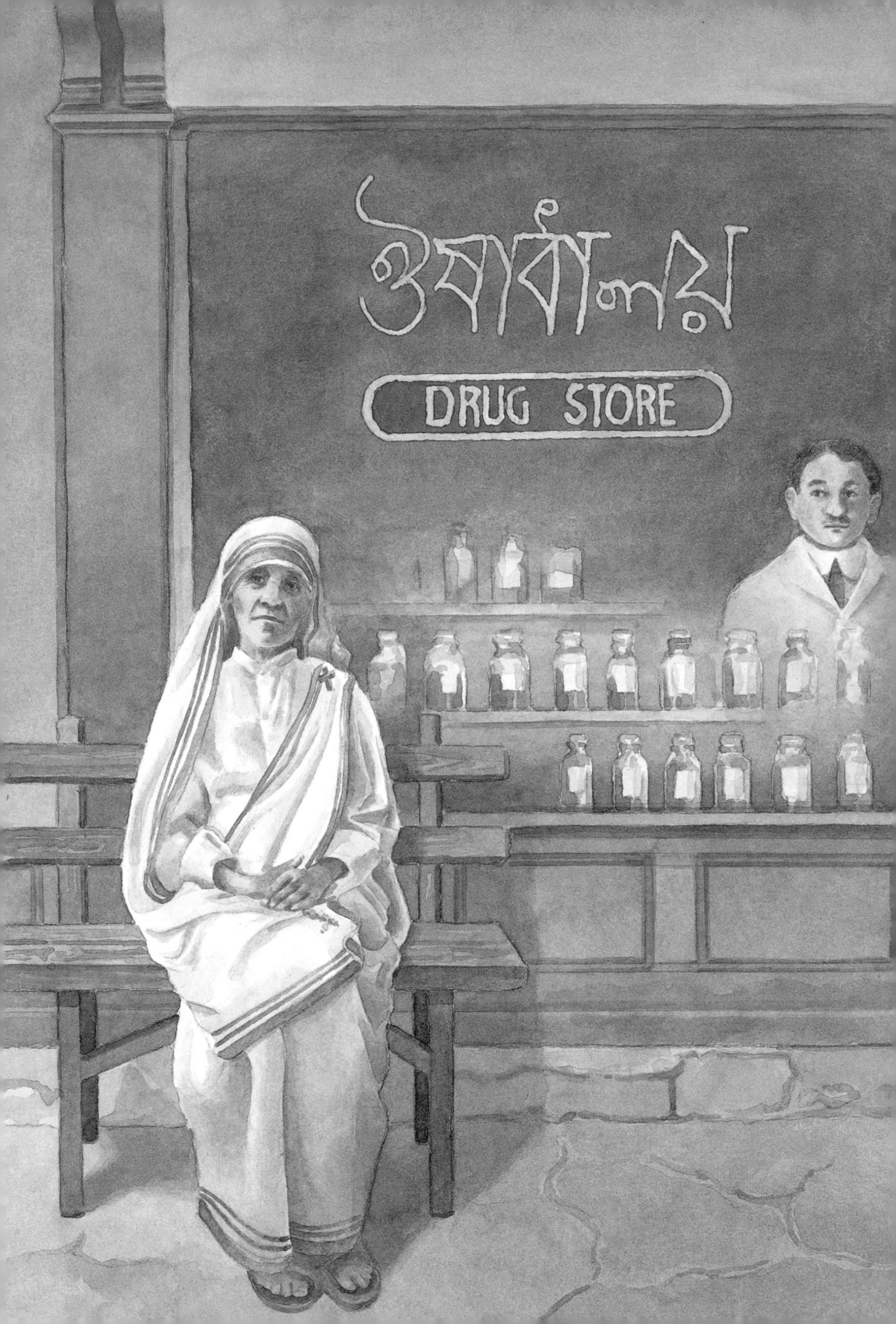
DRUG STORE

Every day, Sister Teresa went

into the slums.

She believed help would come to her.

One day, she needed medicine for the poor.

So Sister Teresa went to a drugstore.

The druggist said

he couldn't give her anything for free.

Sister Teresa sat there all day.

When the shop closed, the druggist

gave her everything on her list.

Soon, two of her old students joined her.

They rented a hut for her school.

Sister Teresa started her own order,

her own group of nuns.

It was called the Missionaries of Charity.

As head of her own order,

she became Mother Teresa.

In 1953, Mother Teresa and her nuns
moved into a big house.
They called it the Mother House.
The sisters rose at 4:45 in the morning.
They prayed and ate breakfast.
Then they cleaned the house.
From 8:00 to 12:30,
the sisters worked in the slums.
They came back to the Mother House
for lunch and rest.
Then they went back on the streets
and worked until 7:30.
Before bed, they ate dinner and prayed.
It was a full, busy day.
Mother Teresa worked all day, too,
but she also worked late into the night.

One day, Mother Teresa found
a dying woman in the gutter.
She carried the woman to a hospital.
But the hospital wouldn't let her in.
There were too many dying people,
they said.

Slum children had schools,
but sick people still died in the streets.
Why shouldn't the dying have loving care?
So Mother Teresa opened a house
called Nirmal Hriday, or "Pure Heart."
No more people would have to die alone.

The days were long,

but Mother Teresa always had time

to wipe one more fevered brow.

She had time to say one more prayer.

She loved babies and the elderly.

She loved the sick and the dying.

And she loved the poorest of the poor.

There was only one Mother Teresa.

She was the woman who believed

every person counts.

Afterword

In 1979, Mother Teresa won the Nobel Peace Prize. Wearing her simple sari, Mother Teresa accepted the award for the poor. She refused the banquet in her honor. She asked that the money be sent to the Missionaries of Charity instead.

As her fame grew, so did her projects. She opened Missionaries of Charity houses all over the world.

One September evening in 1997, the bell tolled at the Mother House. Thousands of people gathered sadly in the streets. At age 87, Mother Teresa was dead.

Her work lives on. There are more than 4,500 sisters and brothers working in Missionaries of Charity houses in 126 countries. The poor and the sick will always have a place to go for help. They will always have people who care for them.

Important Dates

August 26, 1910—Agnes Bojaxhiu is born in Skopje,
Albania.

1919—Agnes's father dies.

1922—Agnes receives her first call from God.

1928—Agnes travels to Ireland to join the Order of the
Sisters of Loreto.

1929—Agnes arrives in Calcutta, India.

1931—Agnes takes her first vows as a nun and takes
the name of Sister Teresa.

1937—Sister Teresa takes her final vows.

1946—Sister Teresa receives her second call from
God.

1948—Sister Teresa leaves Loreto Convent.

1950—Missionaries of Charity created, and Sister
Teresa becomes Mother Teresa.

1952—Mother Teresa founds Nirmal Hriday.

1979—Mother Teresa is awarded the Nobel Peace
Prize.

September 6, 1997—Mother Teresa dies at the Mother
House in Calcutta.